Making Money on YouTube: A Step-by-Step Guide
INTRODUCTION

Welcome to "Making Money on YouTube: A Step-by-Step Guide" - the ultimate resource for anyone looking to turn their passion for creating videos into a profitable business on the world's largest video-sharing platform.

With over two billion monthly active users and over one billion hours of content watched every day, YouTube presents an unparalleled opportunity for creators to reach a global audience and earn a substantial income. However, the road to success on YouTube is not always easy or straightforward.

This comprehensive guide is designed to help you navigate the many challenges and pitfalls of building a successful YouTube channel, and provide you with the tools and strategies you need to start monetizing your content and building a sustainable business on the platform.

Whether you're an aspiring YouTuber looking to get started, or an experienced creator seeking to take your channel to the next level, this guide has something for everyone. From developing a content strategy and building an engaged audience, to monetizing your videos through advertising and sponsorships, we'll cover everything you need to know to succeed on YouTube.

So let's get started on this exciting journey and learn how to turn your passion for video creation into a profitable and rewarding career on YouTube.

INDEX

1. Ad revenue: YouTube pays you a portion of the ad revenue generated by your videos.

1. Sponsorships: You can work with brands to promote their products or services in your videos.
1. Affiliate marketing: You can include affiliate links in your video descriptions and earn a commission on any resulting sales.
1. Merchandise: You can sell merchandise related to your channel, such as t-shirts or mugs.
1. Fan funding: Viewers can donate money directly to your channel through platforms like Patreon or Buy Me a Coffee.
1. Crowdfunding: You can launch a crowdfunding campaign to raise money for a specific project or goal.
1. Super Chat: Viewers can pay to have their comments highlighted during a live stream.
1. YouTube Premium revenue: You can earn a portion of the subscription revenue from YouTube Premium members who watch your videos.
1. Brand deals: You can work with brands to create sponsored content that promotes their products or services.
1. Product reviews: You can review products and earn a fee for your review.
1. Live performances: You can perform music, comedy or other acts on your channel and earn money through ticket sales or tips.
1. Public speaking: You can be invited to speak at events and earn money for your appearance.
1. Licensing: You can license your videos to other media outlets, such as TV shows or websites.

1. Consulting: You can offer consulting services to other creators or businesses looking to grow their YouTube presence.
1. YouTube channel management: You can manage other creators' channels and earn a percentage of their ad revenue.
1. YouTube channel coaching: You can coach other creators on how to improve their channels and earn a fee for your services.
1. YouTube SEO services: You can offer SEO (search engine optimization) services to help other creators improve the discoverability of their videos.
1. Content creation services: You can offer services such as video editing or script writing to other creators or businesses.
1. Guest appearances: You can appear as a guest on other creators' channels and promote your own channel or products.
1. Speaking engagements: You can be hired to speak at conferences or events on topics related to YouTube or social media marketing

Chapter 1
Ad revenue: YouTube pays you a portion of the ad revenue generated by your videos

One of the primary ways to make money on YouTube is through ad revenue. When you monetize your videos, YouTube will display ads on your content and pay you a portion of the revenue generated by those ads. In this summary, we'll explore how ad revenue works on YouTube and how you can maximize your earnings from it.

To start earning ad revenue on your channel, you'll need to meet YouTube's Partner Program requirements. This includes having at least 1,000 subscribers and 4,000 watch hours in the past 12 months, as well as complying with YouTube's community guidelines and terms of service.

Once you've met these requirements, you can apply to join the YouTube Partner Program. If accepted, you'll be able to monetize your videos and start earning money from ad revenue.

Ad revenue is generated when an advertiser chooses to run an ad on your video. YouTube works with advertisers to place ads on videos that are relevant to their target audience. The advertiser pays YouTube for the ad, and YouTube pays you a portion of that revenue.

There are several types of ads that can run on your videos:

Pre-roll ads: These ads run before your video starts and can be skipped after a few seconds.

Mid-roll ads: These ads run during your video and can also be skipped.

Post-roll ads: These ads run after your video has ended and can be skipped.

Overlay ads: These ads appear as banners at the bottom of your video and can be closed by the viewer.

The amount of ad revenue you can earn from your videos depends on several factors, including the type of ad, the advertiser's budget, and the viewer's location. Advertisers may bid more for ads that target a specific audience or geographic location, which can result in higher ad revenue for your videos.

YouTube pays its creators through a program called Google AdSense. AdSense allows you to monetize your content on YouTube and other Google platforms, such as your website or blog. To set up AdSense, you'll need to create an account and link it to your YouTube channel.

Once you've linked your AdSense account to your YouTube channel, you can start earning money from ad revenue. YouTube pays its creators on a monthly basis, typically around the 21st of each month. You can track your earnings in your AdSense account and see how much money you're making from ad revenue.

The amount of money you can earn from ad revenue varies widely depending on your channel's niche, audience, and the type of ads that are running on your videos. Some channels earn just a few dollars per month, while others can earn tens of thousands of dollars or more.

To maximize your earnings from ad revenue, there are several things you can do:

Create high-quality content that is engaging and relevant to your audience. The more views and engagement your videos receive, the more ad revenue you'll earn.

Optimize your videos for search engines by including keywords in your titles, tags, and descriptions. This can help your videos rank higher in search results and attract more viewers.

Promote your videos on social media and other platforms to drive more traffic to your channel.

Encourage viewers to subscribe to your channel and turn on notifications so they don't miss any new videos.

Use YouTube's analytics tools to track your performance and identify areas where you can improve.

Consider partnering with other creators or brands to reach new audiences and increase your exposure.

Test different types of ads and ad placements to see what works best for your channel.

Ad revenue is just one way to make money on YouTube, but it can be a significant source of income for creators who are able to build a large and engaged audience.

Chapter 2

Sponsorships: You can work with brands to promote their products or services in your videos

Another way to make money on YouTube is through sponsorships. Sponsorships are partnerships with brands where you promote their products or services in your videos in exchange for compensation. In this summary, we'll explore how sponsorships work on YouTube and how you can start working with brands to earn money.

To get started with sponsorships, you'll need to have a sizable and engaged audience on your channel. Brands are looking for creators who have a loyal following and can help promote their products or services to a targeted audience.

One of the best ways to attract sponsorships is to create high-quality content that is relevant to your audience. This will help you build a loyal following and establish yourself as an authority in your niche. You should also focus on growing your channel and engaging with your audience through comments, social media, and other channels.

Once you have a significant following, you can start reaching out to brands or wait for them to approach you. Many brands have influencer marketing programs where they work with creators to promote their products or services. You can also sign up for influencer marketing platforms like FameBit, Grapevine, or AspireIQ, which connect brands with influencers.

When working with brands, it's important to disclose your sponsorships to your audience. This is required by the Federal Trade Commission (FTC) and helps ensure transparency and trust between you and your audience. You can do this by including a statement like "This video is sponsored by [Brand]" at the beginning of your video or in the video description.

The compensation you receive for sponsorships can vary widely depending on the brand and the type of sponsorship. Some brands may offer a flat fee for a single video, while others may offer ongoing sponsorships or revenue sharing agreements. You should also consider the value of the products or services you're promoting, as well as any additional benefits like exposure or promotion from the brand.

To maximize your earnings from sponsorships, there are several things you can do:

Build relationships with brands by reaching out to them directly or through influencer marketing platforms.
Create high-quality sponsored content that is relevant to your audience and aligns with your brand values.
Promote your sponsored content on social media and other channels to increase exposure and engagement.
Offer additional value to brands by providing detailed analytics and insights on the performance of your sponsored content.
Build trust and transparency with your audience by disclosing your sponsorships and being upfront about your relationship with the brand.
Negotiate fair compensation for your sponsorships based on the value you provide to the brand.
Sponsorships can be a lucrative way to make money on YouTube, but it's important to choose brands and products that align with your values and are relevant to your audience. You should also be transparent and honest with your audience about your sponsorships to maintain their trust and loyalty.
In addition to sponsorships, there are other ways to make money on YouTube, including merchandise sales, crowdfunding, and affiliate marketing. Merchandise sales involve selling branded products like t-shirts, hats, or mugs to your audience. Crowdfunding involves asking your audience to contribute to a project or goal, often through platforms like Patreon or Kickstarter. Affiliate marketing involves promoting products or services and earning a commission on any sales made through your unique affiliate link.
Overall, making money on YouTube requires hard work, dedication, and a commitment to creating high-quality content that resonates with your audience. By exploring different monetization options and experimenting with different strategies, you can build a sustainable income stream from your YouTube channel

Chapter 3
Affiliate marketing: You can include affiliate links in your video descriptions and earn a commission on any resulting sales

Affiliate marketing is another way to make money on YouTube. It involves promoting products or services and earning a commission on any sales made through your unique affiliate link. In this summary, we'll explore how affiliate marketing works on YouTube and how you can start using it to earn money.

To get started with affiliate marketing, you'll need to sign up for affiliate programs that are relevant to your channel and your audience. There are many affiliate programs available, including Amazon Associates, Clickbank, and Commission Junction. You can also sign up for affiliate programs directly through individual brands or companies.

Once you're signed up for an affiliate program, you can include affiliate links in your video descriptions or in the video itself. These links are unique to you and track any sales made through them. When someone clicks on your affiliate link and makes a purchase, you earn a commission on that sale.

To be successful with affiliate marketing, it's important to promote products or services that are relevant to your audience and align with your brand values. You should also disclose your affiliate links to your audience to ensure transparency and build trust.

When promoting products through affiliate links, it's important to provide value to your audience. This can be done by creating informative and engaging content that showcases the product or service and how it can benefit your audience. You should also be honest and transparent in your reviews and only promote products that you believe in and have personally used.

The compensation you receive for affiliate marketing can vary depending on the affiliate program and the type of product or service being promoted. Some programs offer a percentage of the sale, while others offer a flat fee or a combination of both. It's important to understand the compensation structure before promoting products to ensure that it aligns with your goals and expectations.

To maximize your earnings from affiliate marketing, there are several things you can do:

Choose affiliate programs and products that are relevant to your audience and align with your brand values.

Create high-quality and informative content that showcases the product or service and provides value to your audience.

Disclose your affiliate links to your audience to ensure transparency and build trust.

Promote your affiliate links through various channels, including social media, email newsletters, and other marketing strategies.

Test and experiment with different products and strategies to find what works best for your audience and your goals.

Continuously evaluate the performance of your affiliate marketing efforts and make adjustments as needed.

Affiliate marketing can be a great way to monetize your YouTube channel and earn passive income. However, it's important to approach it with authenticity and integrity to maintain trust and credibility with your audience.

In addition to affiliate marketing, there are other ways to make money on YouTube, including sponsorships, ad revenue, merchandise sales, and crowdfunding. To build a sustainable income stream from your YouTube channel, it's important to explore different monetization options and experiment with different strategies to find what works best for you and your audience.

Overall, making money on YouTube requires hard work, dedication, and a commitment to creating high-quality content that resonates with your audience. By exploring different monetization options and experimenting with different strategies, you can build a sustainable income stream from your YouTube channel

Chapter 4

Merchandise: You can sell merchandise related to your channel, such as t-shirts or mugs

Selling merchandise is another way to make money on YouTube. It involves creating and selling products that are related to your channel, such as t-shirts, mugs, and other items that feature your logo or branding. In this summary, we'll explore how selling merchandise works on YouTube and how you can start using it to earn money.

To get started with selling merchandise on YouTube, you'll need to create a design or logo that represents your channel and brand. This can be done by working with a designer or by creating the design yourself using graphic design software.

Once you have a design, you can use a print-on-demand service such as Teespring, Spreadshirt, or Redbubble to create and sell your merchandise. These services allow you to upload your design and choose the products you want to sell, such as t-shirts, hoodies, mugs, or phone cases. The print-on-demand service will handle the manufacturing, shipping, and customer service for your merchandise, leaving you free to focus on creating content for your channel.

To be successful with selling merchandise on YouTube, it's important to create designs that resonate with your audience and align with your brand values. You should also promote your merchandise through various channels, such as social media, email newsletters, and other marketing strategies. When selling merchandise, it's important to provide high-quality products and excellent customer service to ensure customer satisfaction and build brand loyalty. You should also price your merchandise competitively and consider offering promotions or discounts to incentivize purchases. The compensation you receive for selling merchandise can vary depending on the print-on-demand service and the products being sold. Some services offer a fixed royalty fee for each product sold, while others offer a percentage of the sale price. It's important to understand the compensation structure before selling merchandise to ensure that it aligns with your goals and expectations.

To maximize your earnings from selling merchandise, there are several things you can do:

Create high-quality and attractive designs that resonate with your audience and align with your brand values.

Promote your merchandise through various channels, such as social media, email newsletters, and other marketing strategies.

Provide high-quality products and excellent customer service to ensure customer satisfaction and build brand loyalty.

Price your merchandise competitively and consider offering promotions or discounts to incentivize purchases.

Continuously evaluate the performance of your merchandise sales and make adjustments as needed.

Selling merchandise can be a great way to monetize your YouTube channel and build brand awareness. However, it's important to approach it with authenticity and integrity to maintain trust and credibility with your audience.

In addition to selling merchandise, there are other ways to make money on YouTube, including sponsorships, ad revenue, affiliate marketing, and crowdfunding. To build a sustainable income stream from your YouTube channel, it's important to explore different monetization options and experiment with different strategies to find what works best for you and your audience.

Overall, making money on YouTube requires hard work, dedication, and a commitment to creating high-quality content that resonates with your audience. By exploring different monetization options and experimenting with different strategies, you can build a sustainable income stream from your YouTube channel

Chapter 5
Fan funding: Viewers can donate money directly to your channel through platforms like Patreon or Buy Me a Coffee

Fan funding, also known as crowdfunding or donation-based monetization, is another way to make money on YouTube. It involves soliciting direct financial support from viewers who appreciate your content and want to help you continue creating it. In this summary, we'll explore how fan funding works on YouTube and how you can start using it to earn money.

To get started with fan funding on YouTube, you'll need to set up a profile on a crowdfunding platform such as Patreon, Buy Me a Coffee, or Ko-fi. These platforms allow you to create a page where viewers can donate money in exchange for various rewards and perks, such as exclusive content, behind-the-scenes access, or merchandise.

To encourage viewers to donate, it's important to create compelling rewards that align with your brand and offer genuine value to your supporters. You should also promote your crowdfunding page through various channels, such as social media, email newsletters, and other marketing strategies.

When using fan funding, it's important to be transparent about how the money will be used and to provide regular updates to your supporters. You should also thank your supporters and make them feel appreciated to build a strong community around your channel.

The compensation you receive from fan funding can vary depending on the platform and the number of supporters you have. Some platforms charge a percentage of the donations as a fee, while others offer a fixed monthly fee or no fee at all. It's important to understand the compensation structure before using fan funding to ensure that it aligns with your goals and expectations.

To maximize your earnings from fan funding, there are several things you can do:

Create compelling rewards that align with your brand and offer genuine value to your supporters.

Promote your crowdfunding page through various channels, such as social media, email newsletters, and other marketing strategies.

Be transparent about how the money will be used and provide regular updates to your supporters.

Thank your supporters and make them feel appreciated to build a strong community around your channel.

Continuously evaluate the performance of your crowdfunding page and make adjustments as needed.

Fan funding can be a great way to monetize your YouTube channel and build a loyal community of supporters.

However, it's important to approach it with authenticity and integrity to maintain trust and credibility with your audience. In addition to fan funding, there are other ways to make money on YouTube, including sponsorships, ad revenue, affiliate marketing, and selling merchandise. To build a sustainable income stream from your YouTube channel, it's important to explore different monetization options and experiment with different strategies to find what works best for you and your audience.

Overall, making money on YouTube requires hard work, dedication, and a commitment to creating high-quality content that resonates with your audience. By exploring different monetization options and experimenting with different strategies, you can build a sustainable income stream from your YouTube channel

Chapter 6

Crowdfunding: You can launch a crowdfunding campaign to raise money for a specific project or goal

Crowdfunding is another way to make money on YouTube. It involves launching a fundraising campaign to collect money from a large number of people, often through a dedicated website or platform. In this summary, we'll explore how crowdfunding works on YouTube and how you can use it to raise money for your channel or a specific project.

To get started with crowdfunding on YouTube, you'll need to choose a crowdfunding platform such as Kickstarter, Indiegogo, or GoFundMe. These platforms allow you to create a campaign page where you can showcase your project or goal, explain why it's important, and set a fundraising target. You can also offer rewards to backers who contribute to your campaign, such as exclusive merchandise, early access to your content, or personalized shoutouts.

To make your crowdfunding campaign successful, it's important to create a compelling pitch that resonates with your audience and clearly communicates the value of your project or goal. You should also promote your campaign through various channels, such as social media, email newsletters, and other marketing strategies. It's also important to set realistic fundraising targets and offer rewards that align with the amount of money you're trying to raise.

When using crowdfunding, it's important to be transparent about how the money will be used and to provide regular updates to your backers. You should also thank your backers and make them feel appreciated to build a strong community around your campaign.

The compensation you receive from crowdfunding can vary depending on the platform and the success of your campaign. Some platforms charge a percentage of the donations as a fee, while others offer a fixed monthly fee or no fee at all. It's important to understand the compensation structure before using crowdfunding to ensure that it aligns with your goals and expectations.

To maximize your earnings from crowdfunding, there are several things you can do:

Create a compelling pitch that resonates with your audience and clearly communicates the value of your project or goal.

Promote your campaign through various channels, such as social media, email newsletters, and other marketing strategies.

Be transparent about how the money will be used and provide regular updates to your backers.

Thank your backers and make them feel appreciated to build a strong community around your campaign.

Continuously evaluate the performance of your campaign and make adjustments as needed.

Crowdfunding can be a great way to raise money for your YouTube channel or a specific project. However, it's important to approach it with authenticity and integrity to maintain trust and credibility with your audience and backers.

In addition to crowdfunding, there are other ways to make money on YouTube, including sponsorships, ad revenue, affiliate marketing, selling merchandise, and fan funding. To build a sustainable income stream from your YouTube channel, it's important to explore different monetization options and experiment with different strategies to find what works best for you and your audience.

Overall, making money on YouTube requires hard work, dedication, and a commitment to creating high-quality content that resonates with your audience. By exploring different monetization options and experimenting with different strategies, you can build a sustainable income stream from your YouTube channel

Chapter 7

Super Chat: Viewers can pay to have their comments highlighted during a live stream

Super Chat is a feature on YouTube that allows viewers to pay to have their comments highlighted during a live stream. In this summary, we'll explore how Super Chat works and how you can use it to make money on YouTube.

When you are hosting a live stream on YouTube, viewers can use the Super Chat feature to pay to have their comments stand out. Super Chat comments are highlighted in bright colours and pinned to the top of the live chat for a period of time, depending on the amount of money paid. This allows viewers to get noticed by the streamer and to stand out among the other comments.

To use Super Chat, viewers must have a YouTube account and a payment method set up. They can then select the Super Chat option during the live stream and choose the amount they want to pay. The amount paid determines the length of time the comment is highlighted, with longer times available for higher payments.

To make the most of Super Chat, it's important to encourage viewers to use the feature during your live streams. You can do this by promoting Super Chat at the beginning of your streams and by acknowledging and thanking viewers who use it. You can also offer incentives for viewers who use Super Chat, such as shoutouts or personalized messages. The amount of money you can make from Super Chat depends on the popularity of your live streams and the engagement of your audience. The more viewers you have, and the more they are willing to pay, the higher your earnings will be. However, it's important to remember that Super Chat is just one of many monetization options available on YouTube and should not be relied on as the sole source of income.

To maximize your earnings from Super Chat, there are several things you can do:

Promote Super Chat at the beginning of your live streams and encourage viewers to use the feature.
Acknowledge and thank viewers who use Super Chat during your streams.
Offer incentives for viewers who use Super Chat, such as shoutouts or personalized messages.
Host engaging live streams that encourage viewer participation and engagement.
Continuously evaluate the performance of your live streams and make adjustments as needed.
In addition to Super Chat, there are other ways to make money on YouTube, including sponsorships, ad revenue, affiliate marketing, selling merchandise, and fan funding. To build a sustainable income stream from your YouTube channel, it's important to explore different monetization options and experiment with different strategies to find what works best for you and your audience.
Overall, Super Chat can be a great way to make money on YouTube during live streams. By promoting the feature and encouraging viewer engagement, you can maximize your earnings and build a stronger community around your channel. However, It's Important to remember that Super Chat should be just one part of your overall monetization strategy and not relied on as the sole source of income

Chapter 8
YouTube Premium revenue: You can earn a portion of the subscription revenue from YouTube Premium members who watch your videos

YouTube Premium is a subscription-based service that offers ad-free viewing, access to exclusive content, and other benefits to its members. As a YouTube creator, you can earn a portion of the subscription revenue from YouTube Premium members who watch your videos. In this summary, we'll explore how YouTube Premium revenue works and how you can use it to make money on YouTube. When YouTube Premium members watch your videos, you earn a portion of the subscription revenue based on how much time they spend watching. The revenue is distributed to creators based on a complex algorithm that takes into account factors such as watch time, engagement, and other metrics. While the exact amount you can earn from YouTube Premium revenue varies depending on several factors, such as your niche, your audience size, and the level of engagement of your audience, it can be a significant source of income for some creators.

To be eligible to earn YouTube Premium revenue, you need to meet certain criteria. You must have a minimum number of subscribers and views, and your channel must be in good standing with YouTube's community guidelines and terms of service. Additionally, your content must be advertiser-friendly and not violate any copyright or other intellectual property laws.

To make the most of YouTube Premium revenue, it's important to create high-quality content that is engaging and relevant to your audience. You should focus on building a loyal following of subscribers who are likely to watch your videos and engage with your content. This can be achieved by creating content that is informative, entertaining, and valuable to your audience, and by engaging with your viewers through comments and social media.

Another way to increase your YouTube Premium revenue is to participate in the YouTube Partner Program (YPP). YPP is a program that allows creators to monetize their content through various means, including ad revenue, channel memberships, and Super Chat. To be eligible for YPP, you need to have at least 1,000 subscribers and 4,000 watch hours in the past 12 months. Once you are accepted into the program, you can start earning YouTube Premium revenue along with other monetization options.

It's important to note that YouTube Premium revenue is just one of several ways to make money on YouTube, and it should not be relied on as the sole source of income. You should explore other monetization options, such as sponsorships, affiliate marketing, and merchandise sales, to diversify your income streams and reduce your reliance on any one source of revenue.

To maximize your earnings from YouTube Premium revenue, there are several things you can do:

Create high-quality content that is engaging and relevant to your audience.

Build a loyal following of subscribers who are likely to watch your videos and engage with your content.

Participate in the YouTube Partner Program to unlock additional monetization options.

Continuously evaluate the performance of your videos and make adjustments as needed.

Explore other monetization options to diversify your income streams.

In conclusion, YouTube Premium revenue can be a significant source of income for creators who create high-quality content and have a loyal following of subscribers. By participating in the YouTube Partner Program and building a strong community around your channel, you can maximize your earnings from YouTube Premium revenue and other monetization options. However, it's important to remember that YouTube Premium revenue should be just one part of your overall monetization strategy and not relied on as the sole source of income

Chapter 9

Brand deals: You can work with brands to create sponsored content that promotes their products or services

Brand deals are a popular way for YouTube creators to make money by working with brands to create sponsored content that promotes their products or services. In this summary, we'll explore how brand deals work on YouTube, how to find brand deals, and best practices for creating sponsored content.

A brand deal is a partnership between a creator and a brand where the creator promotes the brand's product or service in exchange for payment or other benefits. Brand deals can take many forms, such as sponsored videos, product placements, sponsored social media posts, and more.

To find brand deals, you need to first build a strong brand and audience around your YouTube channel. Brands are interested in working with creators who have a loyal following of engaged viewers who are likely to be interested in their product or service. You can also reach out to brands directly or work with agencies that specialize in connecting creators with brands.

When creating sponsored content, it's important to be transparent with your viewers and clearly disclose that the content is sponsored. This can be done through verbal or written disclosures in the video, in the video description, or through the use of hashtags such as #ad or #sponsored. Failure to disclose sponsored content can result in violations of advertising laws and regulations, and damage to your credibility with your viewers.

To create effective sponsored content, it's important to focus on providing value to your viewers while also promoting the brand's product or service. This can be achieved by incorporating the brand's product or service in a way that is natural and authentic to your channel's niche and audience. For example, a beauty YouTuber could promote a new makeup line by creating a tutorial using the brand's products, while a travel YouTuber could promote a travel insurance company by creating a video on the importance of travel insurance.

Another best practice for creating sponsored content is to work with brands that align with your values and brand. It's important to work with brands that you believe in and that fit with your niche and audience. This will help ensure that your sponsored content feels authentic and genuine to your viewers.

When negotiating brand deals, it's important to consider factors such as the scope of work, compensation, and exclusivity. The scope of work includes details such as the type and amount of content that you'll be creating for the brand, while compensation can include payment, products, or other benefits. Exclusivity refers to whether or not you'll be able to work with other brands in the same industry or niche during the duration of the brand deal.

In conclusion, brand deals are a popular way for YouTube creators to make money by working with brands to create sponsored content that promotes their products or services. To find brand deals, you need to build a strong brand and audience around your channel and be transparent with your viewers about sponsored content. When creating sponsored content, it's important to focus on providing value to your viewers while also promoting the brand's product or service. Additionally, it's important to work with brands that align with your values and brand, and to negotiate terms that are fair and beneficial for both parties

Chapter 10
Product reviews: You can review products and earn a fee for your review

Product reviews are a common way for YouTube creators to earn money by reviewing products and services for their viewers. In this summary, we'll explore how product reviews work on YouTube, how to find review opportunities, and best practices for creating effective reviews.

Product reviews involve the creator reviewing a product or service and sharing their thoughts and opinions with their viewers. Creators can earn money through product reviews by receiving a fee from the brand or company whose product they are reviewing, or through affiliate marketing where they earn a commission on any resulting sales.

To find review opportunities, creators can reach out to brands directly, sign up for affiliate marketing programs, or work with agencies that specialize in connecting creators with brands. It's important to work with reputable brands that align with your niche and audience, and to be transparent with your viewers about the nature of your relationship with the brand.

When creating a product review, it's important to provide an honest and unbiased assessment of the product or service. This means highlighting both the strengths and weaknesses of the product, and providing a fair and balanced review that helps viewers make an informed decision about whether or not to purchase the product. It's also important to disclose any relationships or compensation that may influence the review.

In addition to providing an honest review, it's important to create a review that is engaging and informative for your viewers. This can be achieved by demonstrating the product in action, providing comparisons to similar products, and highlighting the unique features and benefits of the product.

When negotiating product review fees, it's important to consider factors such as the scope of work, compensation, and exclusivity. The scope of work includes details such as the type and amount of content that you'll be creating for the brand, while compensation can include payment, products, or other benefits. Exclusivity refers to whether or not you'll be able to work with other brands in the same industry or niche during the duration of the review agreement.

It's also important to consider the potential impact of the review on your audience and brand. If the product or service is of low quality or does not align with your values or niche, it can damage your credibility with your audience and harm your brand reputation. It's important to carefully consider which products and services to review, and to only work with brands and products that you believe in and that align with your values.

In conclusion, product reviews are a popular way for YouTube creators to earn money by reviewing products and services for their viewers. To find review opportunities, creators can reach out to brands directly, sign up for affiliate marketing programs, or work with agencies that specialize in connecting creators with brands. When creating a product review, it's important to provide an honest and unbiased assessment of the product or service, and to create a review that is engaging and informative for your viewers. Additionally, it's important to carefully consider the potential impact of the review on your audience and brand, and to only work with brands and products that align with your values and niche

Chapter 11

Live performances: You can perform music, comedy or other acts on your channel and earn money through ticket sales or tips

Live performances are a great way for YouTube creators to earn money by sharing their talents with their audience. In this summary, we'll explore how live performances work on YouTube, how to monetize your live performances, and best practices for creating engaging and successful live events. Live performances on YouTube can include a variety of different types of content, including music, comedy, cooking demonstrations, Q&A sessions, and more. To monetize your live performances, you can charge for tickets or accept tips from viewers. There are a variety of different platforms that creators can use to host their live performances, including YouTube's built-in live streaming feature, as well as third-party platforms like Twitch and Patreon.

To create a successful live performance, it's important to plan ahead and promote your event to your audience. This can include creating a compelling title and description for your event, scheduling it in advance, and promoting it through your social media channels and email list. It's also important to create engaging and interactive content that keeps your audience engaged and encourages them to participate in the event.

One way to encourage participation and engagement during your live performance is to interact with your audience in real-time through features like chat and polls. This can help create a sense of community and connection between you and your audience, which can lead to increased loyalty and support.

When it comes to monetizing your live performances, there are a variety of different options available. Charging for tickets or accepting tips from viewers are two of the most common ways to monetize your live events. Additionally, creators can use features like Super Chat and Super Stickers to monetize their live chats and engage with their audience.

To set ticket prices for your live performances, it's important to consider factors like the type of event, the length of the performance, and the size of your audience. You may also want to consider offering different ticket tiers or packages that include additional perks or benefits.

When it comes to accepting tips from viewers, it's important to be transparent about how the money will be used and to thank viewers for their support. You can also consider offering incentives like shoutouts or personalized messages for viewers who tip a certain amount.

In addition to monetizing your live performances, it's important to consider how they fit into your overall content strategy and brand. Live performances can be a great way to connect with your audience and showcase your talents, but they should also align with your niche and values. It's also important to consider the potential impact of live events on your schedule and workflow, and to plan accordingly to ensure that you have enough time to create quality content on a consistent basis.

In conclusion, live performances are a great way for YouTube creators to monetize their talents and engage with their audience in real-time. To monetize your live performances, you can charge for tickets, accept tips, or use features like Super Chat and Super Stickers. To create successful live events, it's important to plan ahead, promote your event to your audience, and create engaging and interactive content. Additionally, it's important to consider how live performances fit into your overall content strategy and brand, and to plan accordingly to ensure that you can create quality content on a consistent basis

Chapter 12

Public speaking: You can be invited to speak at events and earn money for your appearance

Public speaking is a great way for YouTube creators to share their knowledge and expertise with a wider audience while also earning money. In this summary, we'll explore how public speaking works on YouTube, how to monetize your speaking engagements, and best practices for creating successful speaking events.

Public speaking engagements for YouTube creators can come in a variety of different forms, including keynote speeches, panels, workshops, and more. These engagements can range from virtual events to in-person appearances, and can be organized by a variety of different types of organizations, including corporations, non-profits, and universities.

To monetize your public speaking engagements, you can charge a speaking fee or negotiate a contract that includes payment for your time and expenses. The amount you can earn for a speaking engagement will depend on a variety of factors, including your experience, expertise, and the type of event.

One way to find speaking engagements is to network with other creators, industry professionals, and event organizers. You can also use online resources like SpeakerHub or LinkedIn to find speaking opportunities and connect with potential clients.

To create successful speaking events, it's important to prepare and rehearse your content in advance. This can include creating a compelling and relevant topic, preparing slides and other visual aids, and practicing your delivery. You may also want to consider tailoring your content to the specific audience and event, and incorporating interactive elements like Q&A sessions or audience polls.

When it comes to setting your speaking fee, it's important to consider factors like the length of your presentation, the size of the audience, and your level of experience and expertise. You may also want to consider offering different pricing tiers or packages based on the level of customization or preparation required for the event.

Another way to monetize your public speaking engagements is to sell merchandise or products related to your channel or topic. This can include books, courses, or other resources that provide additional value to your audience and help you earn additional revenue.

In addition to monetizing your speaking engagements, it's important to consider how they fit into your overall content strategy and brand. Public speaking can be a great way to establish yourself as a thought leader in your industry and build your audience, but it's important to ensure that your speaking engagements align with your niche and values. You should also consider the potential impact of speaking engagements on your schedule and workflow, and plan accordingly to ensure that you have enough time to create quality content on a consistent basis.

In conclusion, public speaking is a great way for YouTube creators to share their knowledge and expertise with a wider audience while also earning money. To monetize your speaking engagements, you can charge a speaking fee, negotiate a contract that includes payment, or sell merchandise related to your topic. To create successful speaking events, it's important to prepare and rehearse your content in advance, tailor your content to the specific audience and event, and consider incorporating interactive elements like Q&A sessions or audience polls. Additionally, it's important to ensure that your speaking engagements align with your overall content strategy and brand, and to plan accordingly to ensure that you can create quality content on a consistent basis

Chapter 13

Licensing: You can license your videos to other media outlets, such as TV shows or websites

Licensing is another way to make money from your YouTube content. It involves selling the rights to use your videos to other media outlets, such as TV shows, movies, or websites. Licensing agreements can be a great way to earn extra income and gain exposure for your channel.

To license your videos, you'll need to make sure that you own all of the rights to the content. This means that you should have permission from anyone who appears in your videos, and you should have obtained the necessary licenses for any music or other copyrighted material you've used. If you've used third-party content without permission, you may not be able to license your videos or you may have to negotiate a separate agreement with the owner of the content.

Once you've ensured that you own all of the rights to your content, you can start looking for licensing opportunities. There are several ways to go about this:

Contact media outlets directly: If you have a video that you think would be a good fit for a particular TV show, movie, or website, you can reach out to the media outlet directly and pitch your video. Be sure to explain why you think your video would be a good fit, and provide a link to the video so they can check it out.

Use a licensing platform: There are several online platforms that connect content creators with media outlets that are looking for videos to license. Some popular platforms include Jukin Media, Newsflare, and ViralHog. These platforms typically take a commission on any licensing deals they facilitate, but they can be a good way to reach a wider audience.

Hire a licensing agent: If you're serious about licensing your content, you may want to consider hiring a licensing agent to help you navigate the process. A licensing agent can help you identify potential licensing opportunities, negotiate deals, and ensure that you get fair compensation for your content. However, keep in mind that hiring an agent can be expensive, and you'll need to make sure that the potential earnings from licensing are worth the cost.

When licensing your videos, it's important to be clear about the terms of the agreement. You should specify how the video can be used, how long the license is valid for, and how much you'll be paid. You should also consider whether you want to retain any rights to the video, such as the right to use it on your own channel or to license it to other outlets.

Overall, licensing your videos can be a great way to make money from your YouTube content, as well as to gain exposure for your channel. However, it's important to ensure that you own all of the rights to your content and to be clear about the terms of any licensing agreement you enter into. With the right approach, licensing can be a valuable income stream for content creators on YouTube

Chapter 14
Consulting: You can offer consulting services to other creators or

businesses looking to grow their YouTube presence

Consulting is a great way to earn money as a YouTuber, especially if you have experience and expertise in growing your own channel. Many businesses and creators are looking for help in understanding the platform, creating content, and building an audience. Here are some ways you can offer consulting services and earn money:

One-on-one consulting: You can offer one-on-one consulting services to businesses or individuals looking to grow their YouTube presence. You can charge an hourly rate or a flat fee for a set number of consulting sessions.

Group consulting: You can also offer group consulting services, where you work with multiple clients at the same time. This can be more efficient and cost-effective for both you and your clients.

Online courses: You can create and sell online courses on platforms like Udemy or Teachable, teaching others how to succeed on YouTube. This can be a great way to reach a larger audience and earn passive income.

Webinars: You can host webinars on YouTube or other platforms, where you teach others about specific aspects of YouTube growth and monetization. You can charge a fee for attending the webinar, or use it as a way to promote your consulting services.

Speaking engagements: You can speak at conferences or events, sharing your expertise on YouTube growth and monetization. You can charge a fee for your appearance, and also use it as an opportunity to network and promote your consulting services.

When offering consulting services, it's important to have a clear understanding of your value proposition and what you can offer clients. You should also have a clear pricing structure, and be able to clearly communicate what clients can expect from your services.

One of the benefits of offering consulting services is that you can tailor your services to meet the specific needs of your clients. This can include helping them understand how to create compelling content, how to optimize their videos for search, how to grow their audience through social media, and how to monetize their channel.

Another benefit of consulting is that you can work with a wide range of clients, from small businesses to large corporations, and from individual creators to media companies. This can provide you with a diverse range of experiences and opportunities, and also help you build a strong reputation as a YouTube expert.

In order to be successful at consulting, you need to have a strong understanding of the YouTube platform and its various features and tools. You should also have experience growing and monetizing your own channel, and be able to provide examples of your success to potential clients.

It's also important to stay up-to-date with changes to the platform and new trends in content creation and monetization. This can help you provide the most relevant and effective advice to your clients.

In conclusion, consulting is a great way to earn money as a YouTuber, especially if you have experience and expertise in growing your own channel. By offering consulting services, you can help others succeed on the platform while also building your own brand and reputation as a YouTube expert

Chapter 15
YouTube channel management: You can manage other creators' channels and earn a percentage of their ad revenue

YouTube channel management is a service that involves managing and growing a YouTube channel on behalf of someone else. This can include managing content creation, optimization, marketing, and monetization. As a YouTube channel manager, you can help creators and businesses maximize their potential on the platform and earn money in the process.

One of the most common ways to earn money as a YouTube channel manager is through a revenue sharing agreement. In this type of arrangement, you would receive a percentage of the ad revenue generated by the channel you manage. The specific percentage can vary depending on the agreement you make with the channel owner, but it typically ranges from 10% to 30%.

To become a YouTube channel manager, you'll need to have a strong understanding of the platform and its various features. You should be familiar with content creation, optimization, and promotion strategies that can help a channel grow and monetize effectively. Additionally, you should have strong communication skills and be able to work closely with the channel owner to achieve their goals.

One key aspect of YouTube channel management is content creation. As a manager, you may be responsible for producing videos, writing scripts, or overseeing the creative process. This can involve working with the channel owner to develop ideas, writing scripts or outlines, filming and editing videos, and optimizing content for YouTube's algorithms.

Optimizing content for YouTube is another important aspect of channel management. This can include keyword research, optimizing video titles and descriptions, and using analytics to track the performance of videos. You may also need to stay up to date on the latest YouTube trends and algorithm updates to ensure that your channel is always performing at its best.

Marketing and promotion are also important components of YouTube channel management. You may need to create and manage social media accounts for the channel, develop email marketing campaigns, or work with influencers and other creators to promote the channel to new audiences.

As a YouTube channel manager, you can work with a wide range of clients, including individual creators, small businesses, and larger media companies. The specific tasks and responsibilities you take on will depend on the needs and goals of each client, but can include anything from basic content creation and optimization to full-scale channel management and growth strategies.

In terms of earning potential, YouTube channel management can be a lucrative career path. As mentioned earlier, revenue sharing agreements can provide a consistent stream of income for managers who are able to grow and monetize channels effectively. Additionally, some channel managers charge a flat fee or hourly rate for their services, which can vary depending on the level of service provided.

One potential challenge of YouTube channel management is the competitive nature of the industry. With millions of channels on the platform, it can be difficult to stand out and attract new viewers. Additionally, YouTube's constantly evolving algorithms can make it difficult to achieve consistent growth and success.

To overcome these challenges, it's important to stay up to date on the latest trends and best practices in YouTube channel management. This can involve attending industry events and conferences, networking with other managers and creators, and staying active on social media and other online communities.

In summary, YouTube channel management can be a lucrative and rewarding career path for those with a strong understanding of the platform and its various features. By helping creators and businesses grow and monetize their channels, you can earn money while helping others achieve their goals on the platform

Chapter 16

YouTube channel coaching: You can coach other creators on how to improve their channels and earn a fee for your services

YouTube channel coaching is a way to help other creators improve their channels and grow their audience. As a coach, you can offer your expertise and experience to guide others in areas such as video production, audience engagement, and monetization strategies.

To become a YouTube channel coach, you should have a deep understanding of the platform and its features, as well as experience in creating successful content and growing a channel. It's also helpful to have a solid understanding of marketing, branding, and audience psychology.

There are a few ways to offer coaching services. One option is to create and sell online courses or coaching programs that teach creators how to improve their channels. These programs can include pre-recorded video lessons, live coaching sessions, and access to online communities or forums where creators can connect with each other and share their experiences.

Another option is to offer one-on-one coaching services where you work directly with creators to help them improve their channels. This can involve personalized coaching sessions, video critiques, and ongoing support and guidance.

As a YouTube channel coach, you can charge a fee for your services based on your level of expertise and the amount of time and resources you're investing in each client. Some coaches charge a flat fee per session, while others charge a monthly retainer or a percentage of the revenue their clients generate through their channels.

To market your coaching services, you can use social media platforms, such as Twitter, LinkedIn, and Instagram, to promote your expertise and attract potential clients. You can also create educational content, such as blog posts or videos, that showcase your knowledge and skills in specific areas related to YouTube channel management and growth. It's important to note that YouTube has strict policies around paid promotions and endorsements, so it's important to disclose any financial relationships you have with creators you work with. This can include disclosing any fees you receive for coaching services or any affiliate relationships you have with products or services you recommend.

Overall, YouTube channel coaching can be a lucrative and rewarding way to help other creators achieve their goals and grow their channels. It requires a deep understanding of the platform and a commitment to staying up-to-date with the latest trends and best practices, but with the right skills and expertise, it can be a valuable service for creators looking to take their channels to the next level

Chapter 17
YouTube SEO services: You can offer SEO (search engine optimization) services to help other creators improve the discoverability of their videos

YouTube SEO services involve optimizing videos and channels for better search engine rankings and visibility on YouTube. As a YouTube SEO consultant, you can offer your services to other creators who want to improve the performance of their channels. Here is a complete summary of YouTube SEO services and how you can make money from them.

What is YouTube SEO?

YouTube SEO is the process of optimizing your videos and channel to rank higher in YouTube search results. By optimizing your videos for search, you can increase your chances of getting discovered by viewers who are searching for content related to your niche. Some key factors that impact YouTube SEO include keywords, video titles, descriptions, tags, and engagement metrics like views, likes, and comments.

How to make money with YouTube SEO services

Offer keyword research and optimization: As a YouTube SEO consultant, you can offer keyword research and optimization services to help other creators target the right keywords for their content. By identifying high-volume, low-competition keywords, you can help creators improve their visibility and attract more viewers to their channels.

Optimize video titles and descriptions: Video titles and descriptions are critical elements of YouTube SEO. By optimizing titles and descriptions with relevant keywords and compelling language, you can help videos rank higher in search results and attract more clicks.

Improve video tags: Tags are another important aspect of YouTube SEO. By optimizing video tags with relevant keywords and phrases, you can help videos appear in more search results and reach a wider audience.

Boost engagement metrics: Engagement metrics like views, likes, and comments are important indicators of video quality and relevance. By helping creators improve their engagement metrics, you can improve their search rankings and increase their chances of being discovered by new viewers.

Provide channel optimization: In addition to optimizing individual videos, you can also offer channel optimization services to help creators improve the overall performance of their channels. This might include optimizing channel descriptions, cover images, and playlists, as well as analyzing engagement metrics and recommending improvements.

Create custom thumbnails: Custom thumbnails are an important visual element of YouTube SEO. By creating eye-catching thumbnails that accurately represent the content of a video, you can improve click-through rates and attract more viewers to a channel.

Offer analytics and reporting: By tracking key performance metrics like views, watch time, and engagement, you can provide valuable insights to creators about the performance of their videos and channels. You can also offer regular reporting to help creators understand how their channels are growing over time and identify areas for improvement. Develop YouTube advertising campaigns: In addition to organic SEO, you can also offer YouTube advertising services to help creators promote their videos and channels to a wider audience. By creating targeted advertising campaigns that reach the right viewers, you can help creators grow their channels and increase their revenue. Provide ongoing consultation: As a YouTube SEO consultant, you can offer ongoing consultation to help creators stay up-to-date with the latest best practices and trends in YouTube SEO. By staying on top of changes to the YouTube algorithm and offering tailored advice to individual creators, you can build long-term relationships and earn recurring revenue.

In summary, YouTube SEO services offer a range of opportunities to make money as a consultant or service provider. By offering targeted services like keyword research, video optimization, and channel management, you can help other creators improve their visibility and grow their channels. With the right expertise and approach, you can build a successful business offering YouTube SEO services and help creators achieve their goals on the platform.

Chapter 18

Content creation services: You can offer services such as video editing or script writing to other creators or businesses

As a YouTuber, you've likely developed a strong set of skills in video creation, editing, and storytelling. You can leverage these skills to offer content creation services to other creators or businesses.

There are many creators or businesses that don't have the time or expertise to create their own content, but understand the importance of video as a marketing tool. By offering your services, you can help these clients produce high-quality videos that engage their audience and drive results.

There are several types of content creation services you can offer as a YouTuber:

Video editing: Many creators or businesses may have footage but lack the skills or software to edit it effectively. You can offer video editing services to help them create polished and professional-looking videos.

Script writing: Writing a compelling script is a crucial aspect of creating engaging videos. You can offer your scriptwriting services to clients who may have a great idea but need help putting it into words.

Storyboarding: Storyboarding is the process of visually planning out a video before filming. You can offer storyboarding services to help clients plan out their videos and ensure that they're telling a cohesive story.

Motion graphics: Adding motion graphics to a video can make it more engaging and dynamic. You can offer your motion graphics skills to clients who want to make their videos stand out.

Animation: Animation can be a powerful storytelling tool, but it can also be time-consuming and technically challenging. You can offer animation services to clients who want to create animated explainer videos or other types of animation.

When offering content creation services, it's important to have a clear understanding of what the client needs and what you can offer. You should also be upfront about your rates and deliverables so that the client knows exactly what to expect.

To find clients for your content creation services, you can reach out to other YouTubers or businesses in your niche and pitch your services. You can also create a portfolio of your work and share it on your social media channels or website to attract potential clients.

When working with clients, be sure to establish clear communication channels and set expectations from the beginning. You should also have a clear contract or agreement in place that outlines the scope of the project, deadlines, and payment terms.

Offering content creation services can be a great way to diversify your income as a YouTuber. Not only can it help you earn additional income, but it can also help you develop new skills and expand your professional network.

Chapter 19

Guest appearances: You can appear as a guest on other creators' channels and promote your own channel or products

Making guest appearances on other creators' channels is a great way to get more exposure for your own channel and potentially earn some money in the process. By appearing on other channels, you can reach new audiences and gain new subscribers who may be interested in the content on your own channel.

One way to make money through guest appearances is to promote your own products or services during the appearance. For example, if you have a merch line or offer consulting services, you can promote these offerings during the appearance and potentially earn some sales as a result.

Another way to earn money through guest appearances is to charge a fee for your appearance. Some creators may be willing to pay for the opportunity to collaborate with you or have you on their channel. You can negotiate a fee based on the amount of time you'll be spending on their channel, the size of their audience, and the level of promotion you'll be doing for the appearance.

In addition to earning money, guest appearances can also be a great way to build relationships with other creators and potentially collaborate on future projects. By working with other creators in your niche, you can expand your reach and create more opportunities for growth and success.

To find opportunities for guest appearances, start by reaching out to other creators in your niche who have a similar audience to yours. You can also join online communities and groups for creators to connect with others who may be interested in collaborating.

When reaching out to other creators, be sure to pitch your appearance in a way that highlights the value you can bring to their channel. Explain why you would be a good fit for their audience and how you can help them create engaging content. It's also important to be clear about what you're looking for in terms of compensation or promotion for the appearance.

Overall, guest appearances can be a fun and profitable way to grow your channel and connect with other creators in your niche. By putting yourself out there and collaborating with others, you can create new opportunities for success and continue to build your brand and audience on YouTube

Chapter 20

Speaking engagements: You can be hired to speak at conferences or events on topics related to YouTube or social media marketing

One lesser-known way to make money from your YouTube channel is through speaking engagements. As a successful YouTuber, you've likely gained expertise and knowledge on topics related to YouTube and social media marketing, and there may be businesses, conferences, or other events that are willing to pay you to share that knowledge with their audience.

Speaking engagements can be a great way to not only make money, but also to network with other professionals in your industry and gain exposure for your channel. Here are some steps you can take to start securing speaking engagements: Define your niche: Identify the specific topics that you are most knowledgeable about and passionate about. This will help you determine which events or conferences to target and what type of content to focus on in your presentations. Build your expertise: Consider pursuing additional training or certifications related to your niche. This can help you stand out from other potential speakers and increase your credibility in your field.

Create a speaker profile: Put together a professional speaker profile that showcases your expertise, previous speaking experience, and any relevant media appearances. Include testimonials from previous clients or attendees, if possible.

Reach out to event organizers: Start by researching events and conferences related to your niche. Look for opportunities to apply as a speaker, or reach out to event organizers with a pitch for your presentation. Be sure to highlight what makes you unique and why you would be a valuable addition to their lineup of speakers.

Prepare your presentation: Once you've secured a speaking engagement, it's time to start preparing your presentation. Make sure your content is tailored to the specific audience and event, and consider incorporating multimedia elements like video clips or slideshows to make your presentation more engaging.

Promote your speaking engagement: Use your social media channels and email list to promote your upcoming speaking engagement. This can help drive attendance to the event and also showcase your expertise to your followers.

When it comes to pricing your speaking engagements, there are a few factors to consider. First, think about the value that you bring to the event or conference. If you're speaking on a niche topic and have a lot of expertise in that area, you may be able to command a higher fee. Additionally, consider the size and location of the event, as well as the level of competition from other speakers.

Overall, speaking engagements can be a lucrative and rewarding way to make money from your YouTube channel. By leveraging your expertise and networking with other professionals in your industry, you can expand your reach and gain valuable exposure for your brand

www.ingramcontent.com/pod-product-compliance
Lightning Source LLC
Chambersburg PA
CBHW071121220526
45467CB00004B/1993